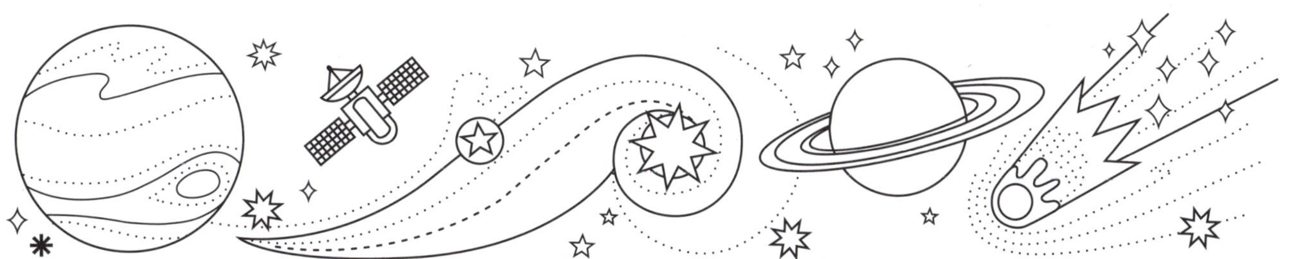

Name

Teacher

School

AF595931

Learning goal: To improve knowledge of the alphabet in NSW Foundation style handwriting

Success criteria:

- I can write all lower-case and capital letters of the alphabet in NSW Foundation style using both printing and cursive.
- I can write in NSW Foundation style legibly, using appropriate slope, spacing and size.

Are you ready to write?

Posture

Ensure your feet are flat on the floor and you are sitting well back in the chair.

Paper position

Hold the paper with your non-writing hand.

left-handed

right-handed

Pencil grip

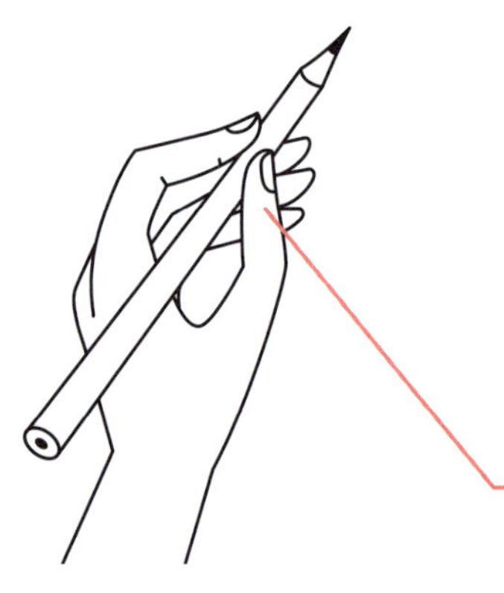

Hold your pencil with one finger on top of the barrel.

Support the barrel with your thumb.

left-handed

right-handed

Foundation printing

Revise your Foundation printing. Match each word to its meaning, then copy the text.

Hydrogen	Stars	Galileo	Orbits	NASA

______ : astronomical bodies that are visible at night and are not planets.

______ : the paths Earth and other planets take around the Sun.

______ : the gas the Sun is mostly made up of.

______ : an Italian astronomer who discovered that the planets revolve around the Sun.

______ : the USA space agency that sent the first person to land on the Moon.

Capital letters

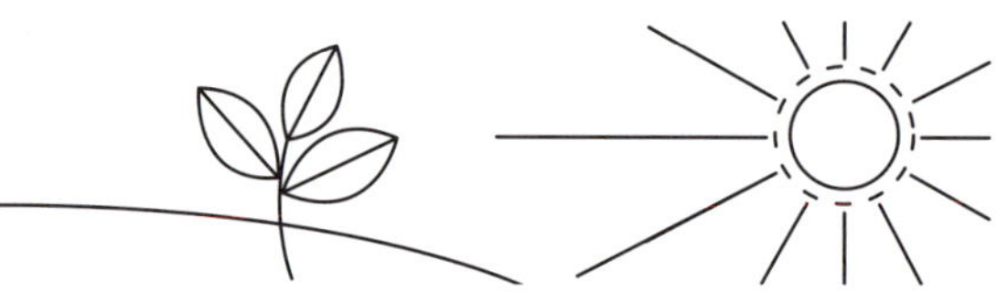

Revise your capital letters.

A B C D E F G H I J K L M N O P

Q R S T U V W X Y Z

Copy the words using all capital letters.

SCIENCE RESEARCH ENERGY ATMOSPHERE

UNIVERSE SOLAR LUNAR FUSION

ECLIPSE ROTATE GRAVITY AXIS

Rewrite these words in all capital letters.

asteroid comet telescope radio waves

satellites terrestrial phases crescent

equinox elliptical transit momentum

velocity gibbous meteor constellation

gas giant nebula exoplanet corona

Numerals

Revise your numerals. Write the missing numerals in the gaps, then copy the text.

Earth is one hundred and fifty million kilometres from the Sun.

= ________________ km

The circumference of Earth is forty thousand and thirty kilometres.

= ________________ km

It takes three hundred and sixty-five days for Earth to orbit

the Sun.

= __________ days

A lunar month, when the Moon changes from a thin crescent

to a full Moon, is about twenty-nine days long.

= ________ days

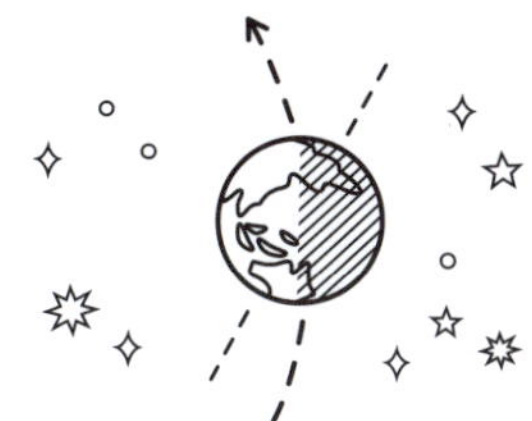

Horizontal joins to 'e'

lower dip

oe re ve we xe

Remember: dip a little lower when making a horizontal join to 'e'.

Copy these words, then underline letter pairs that have a horizontal join to 'e'.

discovered three very travel pressure coexist nowhere

rest powerful adventurer current drive observed

active explore axel relaxed extreme over weather

Practise your horizontal joins to 'e'. Rewrite these words in cursive.

shoe recently arrived several atmosphere

hemisphere structure interest average echoes

Copy the text. Remember to be careful with your horizontal joins to 'e'.

Jupiter is the largest planet in the solar system. Its stripes are made up of ammonia and water. Astronomers believe it might have up to 67 moons. Because it is made up of swirling gases and liquid, Jupiter does not have a solid surface.

Joining 'ft'

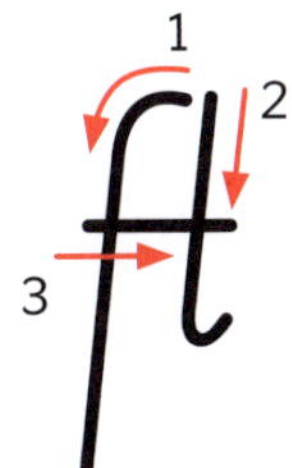

Remember: when joining 'f' to 't', the letters share a crossbar. Add the crossbar last.

Copy these letter pairs.

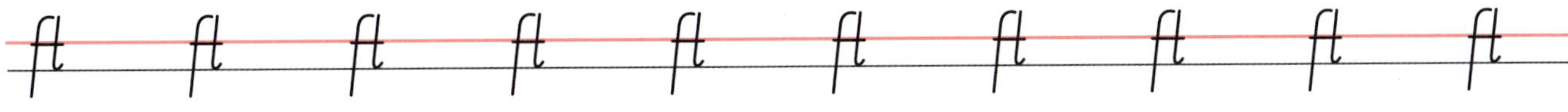

Copy the text. Remember to be careful with your 'ft' joins.

The Apollo 13 mission to the Moon lifted off in 1970. After it left Earth, there was a problem with one of the oxygen tanks in the spacecraft, which endangered the crew. The NASA scientists on Earth worked swiftly to ensure the astronauts landed safely in the Pacific Ocean.

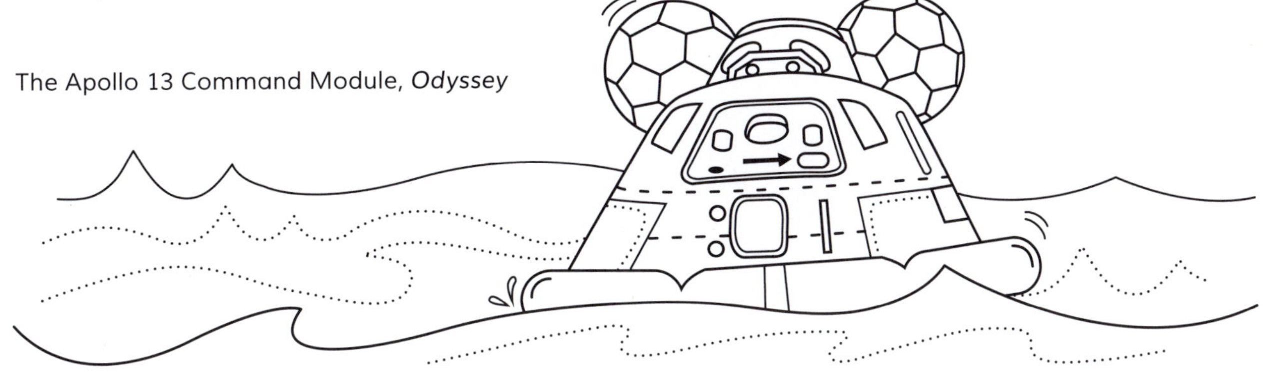

The Apollo 13 Command Module, *Odyssey*

Joining to 's'

as → as

Remember: when joining diagonally to the letter 's', you can modify the shape of the 's' so there is less to retrace.

Copy these words with diagonal joins to 's'.

astronomer phase cluster crescent density comets dust planets

giants Uranus moons skies debris gas sustain acclimatise

Remember: when joining horizontally to 's', the letter 's' doesn't change.

Copy these words with horizontal joins to 's'.

Mars appears close doors windows most oscillate

cosmic expose position drowsy gears torsion purpose

Copy the text.

Astronomers use powerful telescopes to investigate things such as the position of the planets and the density of globular clusters.

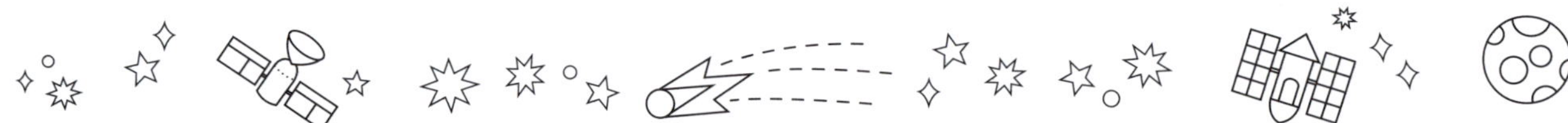

Self-assessment: Tricky joins

Copy the text. Remember to be careful with your tricky joins.

Today, we know that Earth is spherical, but there was a time when it was believed to be flat. Many early maps depict a flat Earth. From our everyday view, Earth looks flat. However, the view of our planet from a spacecraft gives us a more accurate idea of its true shape. Today, scientists analyse photographs taken from satellites in outer space, which enable them to see objects in space very clearly. An image with many pixels even allows astronomers to see tornadoes on the surface of other planets in great detail.

Self-assessment

Rate your tricky joins.

I need more practice.

Good.

Excellent!

Fluency joins from 'b', 'p' and 's'

ba pi se

TIP

Joins from the clockwise finishers 'b', 'p' and 's' are called fluency joins. A fluency join can speed up your handwriting because it doesn't require a pencil lift. Retrace a bit from the bottom of the letter.

Copy these letter pairs with fluency joins.

sc so sy su sm si sp bi br bu

bs by ba be pu pr po pe pi pa

Copy these words with fluency joins.

solar system scientific supergiant space spiral supernova

spectrum suspicious surface smaller synergy superior

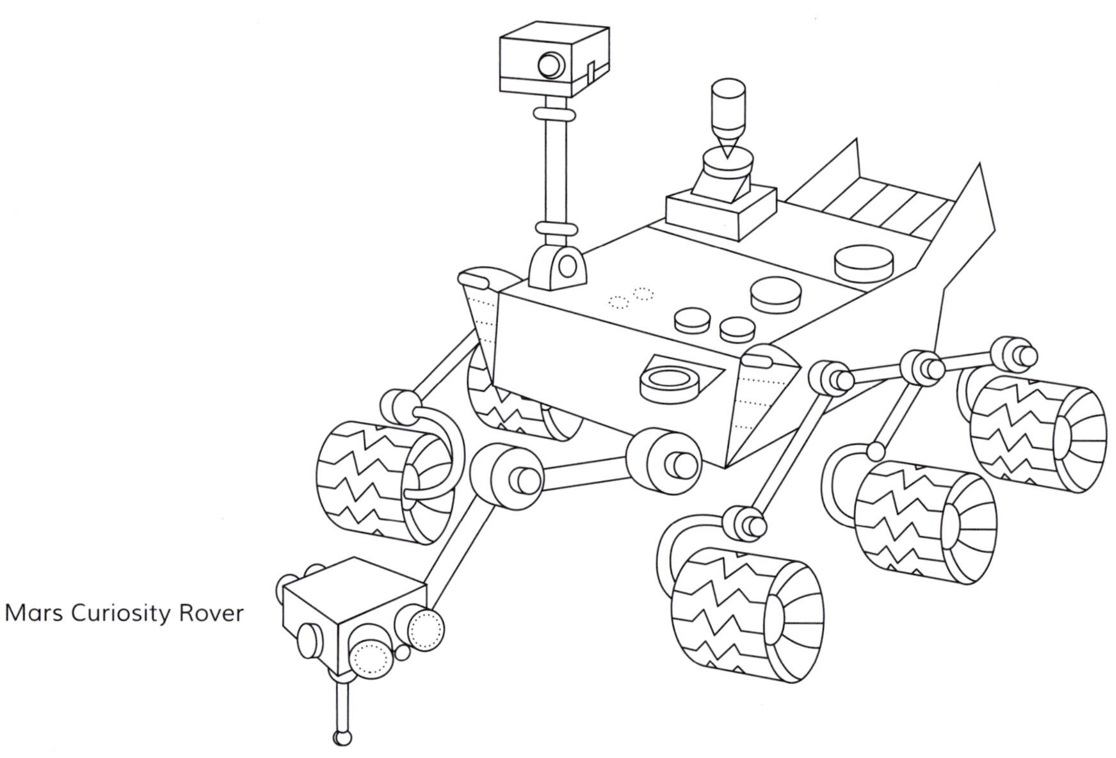

Mars Curiosity Rover

Copy these words with fluency joins.

eclipse pulsar prism quasar isotope telescope emission

density cosmology big bang penumbra binary bolide

binoculars absorb fireball absolute earthbound orbit

polarise primary partial position proton pulsar precede

pixel pupil parallel open eyepiece escape ellipse

Build your own words using fluency joins.

b	+	an	est	at	ake
p		olar	ig	ile	end
s		ill	and	ack	eat

Fluency joins to ascenders

ph st

When making a fluency join from 'b', 'p' or 's', retrace a bit on the way down from the ascender.

Copy these letters pairs with fluency joins to ascenders.

bb bl bt ph pl pt sh sk sl st

bb bl bt ph pl pt sh sk sl st

Copy these words.

shock shower stratosphere shooting star sky stellar

dust solstice starburst stone astronauts terrestrial

protostar cluster celestial storm astronomy interstellar

constellation black hole blanket blue blackened blast

blink Hubble doubtful double bubble planet photon

phase photo plus subtle plasma photometer Neptune

atmosphere elliptical Alpha Centauri ripple optimism

Copy the poem, then complete it by adding three lines of your own. Include as many words as you can from the box.

storm	shower	starburst	dust	blast
blink	planet	Neptune	phase	photo

Celestial Sky

I blink in awe at the beauty of the constellations above me,

A cluster of brightness in the blackened night,

I think of the astronauts who went forth like shooting stars,

Full of bravery and optimism,

I wonder

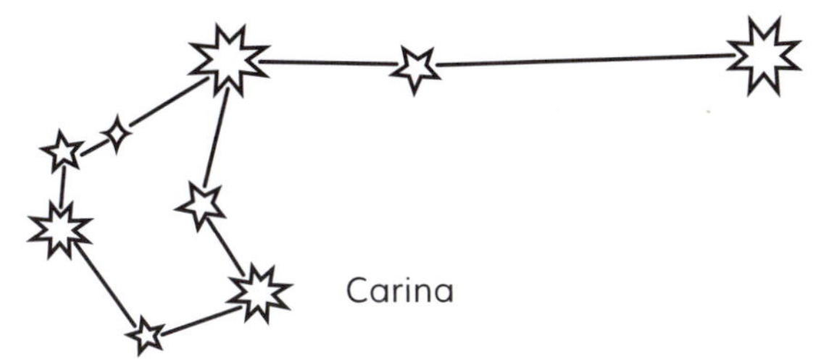
Carina

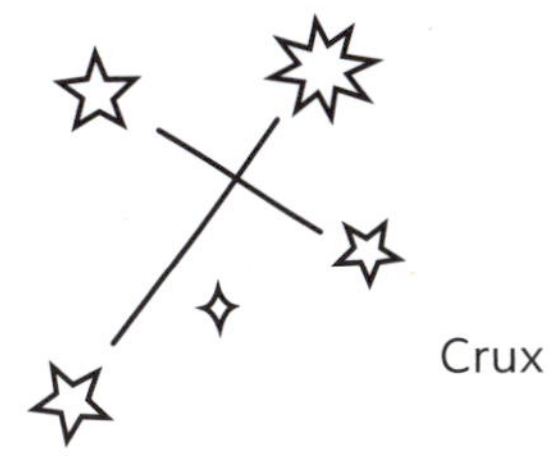
Crux

Practising fluency joins

Copy these words with fluency joins. Rewrite them in alphabetical order.
It may be helpful to cross out each word as you put it in order.

storm planet stratosphere brightest blackened
star supergiant sky stellar Hubble photo shock
photometer solstice starburst stone astronauts
proton fireball terrestrial protostar cluster celestial
magnetosphere interstellar dust constellation
telescope eclipse binoculars
scientific plasma space

a b c d e f g h i j k l m n o p q r s t u v w x y z

Rewrite the text in cursive. Remember to be careful with your fluency joins.

The Commonwealth Scientific and Industrial Research Organisation (CSIRO) is an Australian agency that studies space. It manages several observatories that conduct useful radio astronomy research. CSIRO scientists also track spacecrafts on interplanetary exploration missions. The CSIRO has collaborated with NASA for over 50 years to expand our understanding of the universe.

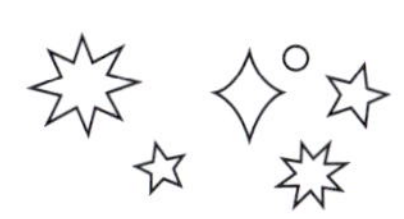
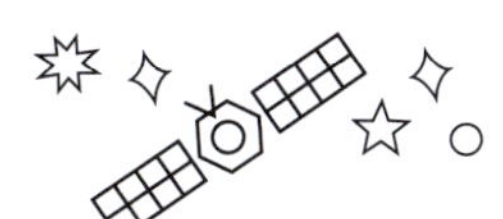

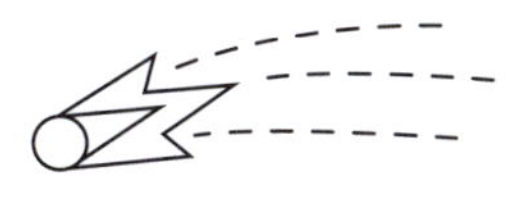

get.ga/PMWA100

ISBN: 9780170416931

Copy the text. Take special care with your fluency joins from 'b', 'p' and 's'.

The Hubble Space Telescope flies above Earth's atmosphere, taking digital photographs that show the position of the clusters of stars in space. It takes photographs of planets, stars and galaxies, and sends them back to Earth through radio waves. NASA launched the telescope from the Kennedy Space Center, Florida, USA, in 1990. The Hubble Space Telescope orbits Earth at a speed of over 27 000 kilometres per hour.

Peer review

Ask your partner to give you some feedback on how well you wrote the text above. Ask them to notice how carefully you completed your fluency joins.

2 stars (two things you did well)

I wish (a way for you to improve)

Slope

How consistent is your slope? Trace and copy these words within the wavy lines, then use a ruler to draw slope lines along the vertical parts of the letters.

Rewrite the words, using the slope lines as a guide.

dust storms iron oxide polar ice caps planet ocean

rings orbit scorching surface hydrogen helium

Spacing

Read the sentence, then write it with even spacing between letters and words.

Cons istent spac ing betw een le tters an d word s

makes you r handwriting eas ier to r ead.

Write each word in the word shapes. If your letter spacing is even, the word will fit in the shape.

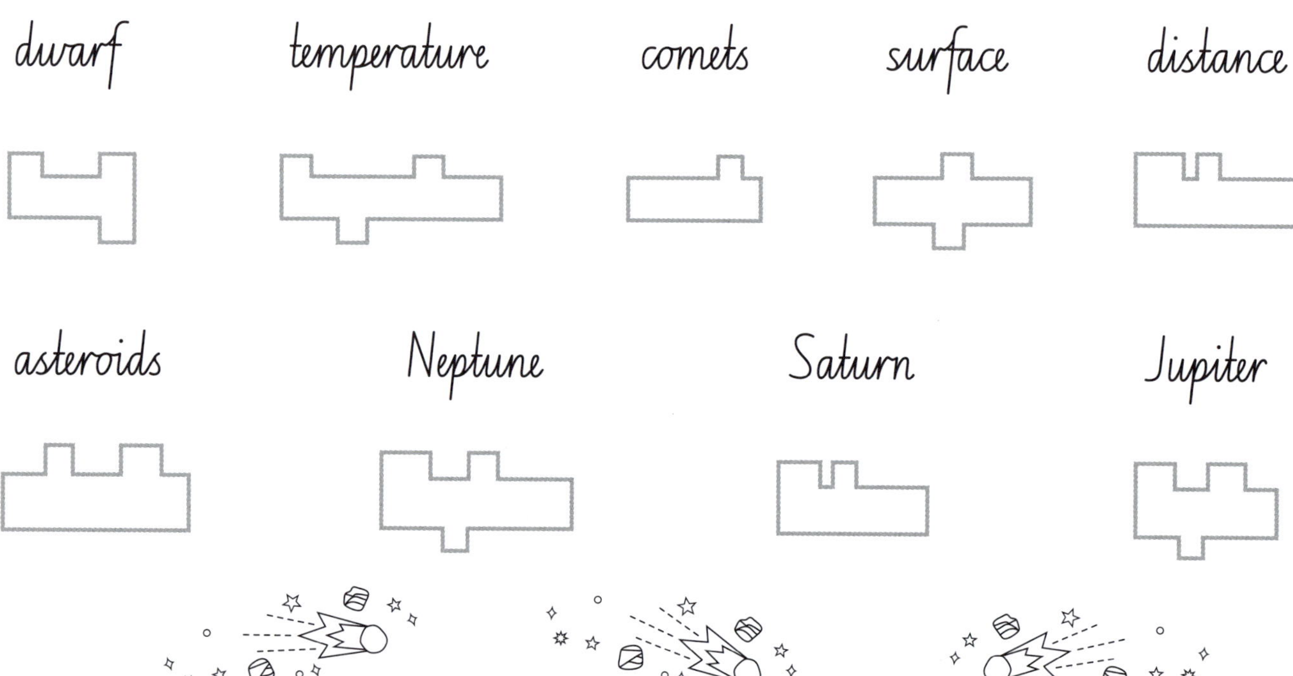

Copy the text, then check your spacing. Colour a small red square between each word.

When the solar system was formed, the leftover material

became asteroids, meteoroids and comets. These orbit the Sun.

A meteor, or shooting star, is a meteoroid that enters Earth's

atmosphere and burns up in a bright blaze of light.

Size

Copy these words in the spaces provided. How much does your handwriting vary in size from the models?

speeds travel gravity energy temperature

atmosphere galaxy moons satellites particles

spiral debris spacecraft formation motion

Sometimes you need to write at a different size. Can you change the size of your writing and maintain your legibility?

space space space space

Write the word 'Mars' in cursive in the word shapes. Use the shapes to help you write at a consistent size.

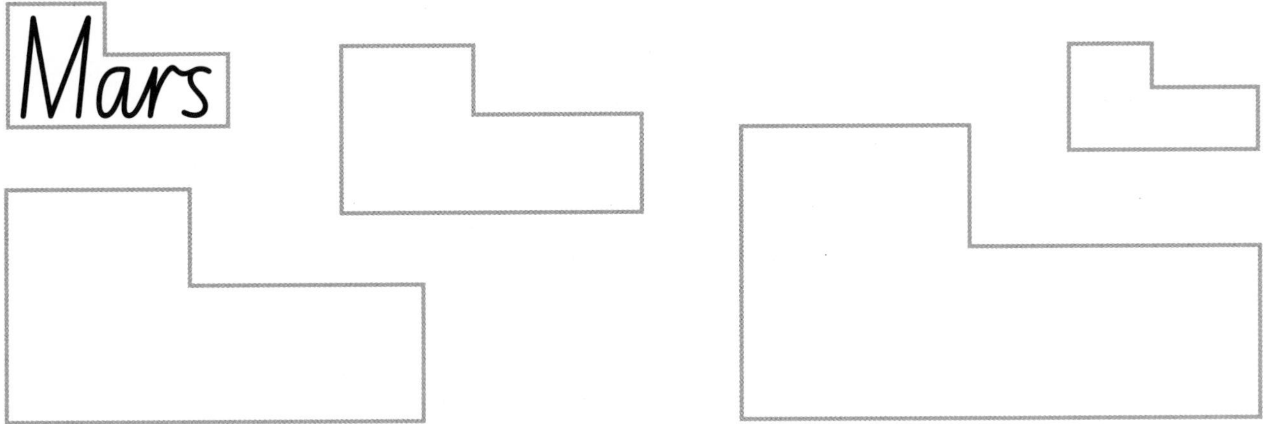

Copy the text. Take special care with your slope, spacing and size.

Saturn, like the other gas giants, Jupiter, Uranus and Neptune, is surrounded by rings. Saturn's rings are very bright and contain lots of material. The rings are actually made up of thousands of ringlets. The band of rings is up to 282 000 km across, but only 1 km thick. The dusty ice particles that make up the rings vary in size from grains to boulders. Scientists have been using the Hubble Space Telescope to learn more about the rings.

Peer review

Ask your partner to give you some feedback on how well you wrote the text above. Ask them to notice how careful you were with your slope, spacing and size.

2 stars (two things you did well)

I wish (a way for you to improve)

Diagonal joins to ascenders

Remember: sweep up and retrace part of the ascender.

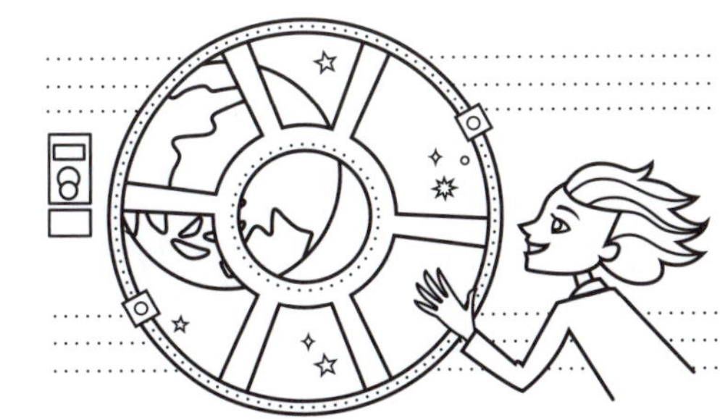

Copy these letter pairs with diagonal joins to ascenders.

ab ak al at cl ch ck ct eb eh el et ib il

it kl lb ll lt mb ml nt nh th tt ul ub ut

Copy these words, paying attention to your diagonal joins to ascenders.

Jupiter telescope aviator fuel terrestrial aviation levitate

astronaut scientist constellation clusters meteor velocity

density Alpha Centauri wavelength giant astronauts

gravity telescopes scientists galactic radiant chart yellow

Hubble Space Telescope shuttle torch burnt celebrity letter

absence allow think bubble cling abstract clues

Diagonal joins from 'q'

Remember: when making a diagonal join from 'q', you need to quickly change direction and go all the way to the top of the next letter.

Copy these 'qu' letter pairs.

qu qu qu qu qu qu qu qu

Copy these words. Remember to be careful with your diagonal joins from 'q'.

equinox quad square squid squash aquatic

queen question squat quill equipment quick

quiet equally quarter quench quotation unique

Copy the text.

Astronomers used to question and study exactly when the equinox would occur. The equinox is when day and night are of equal length. Scientific equipment was also used to research the four phases, or quarters, of the Moon.

Diagonal joins from 'z'

Remember: making a little wave with your pen or pencil will give you the momentum to join to the next letter.

Copy these letter pairs with diagonal joins from 'z'.

zi zo zl zy ze zu zi zo zl zy ze zu

Copy the words. Remember to be careful with your diagonal joins from 'z'.

zodiac zip zoom lazy wheeze zoo zebra zero

hazy dizzy zone ooze zany sizzle zap ablaze

Copy the text.

Have you ever seen a comet zoom across the sky at night? They

are very fast and zippy! They seem to take zero time to move

across the zodiac belt, their bright tails blazing behind them.

Diagonal joins review

Take a letter from each box to make letter pairs with diagonal joins.

ab

a c d e h i k l m n t u	to	b e h i k l m n s t u y z

Copy the phrases, then underline the diagonal joins.

International Space Station

unique place

six people live

occupied since November 2000

conduct research

solar arrays provide power

inside a laboratory

contains observatory module

Make new words by adding a letter or letters to these word endings with diagonal joins.

____ake ____ain ____ate ____ill

____ait ____ail ____ink ____ent

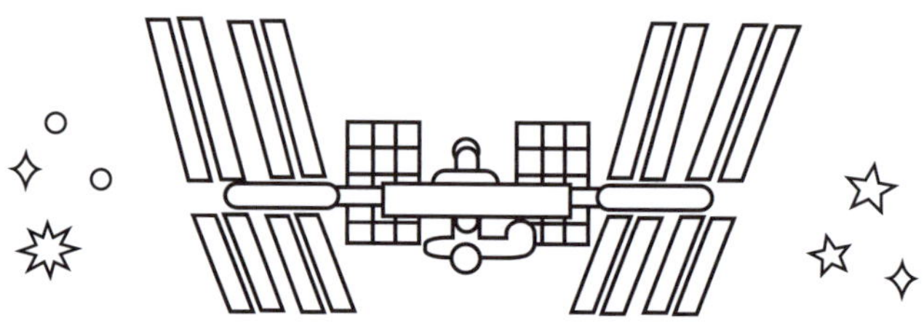

Drop-in joins

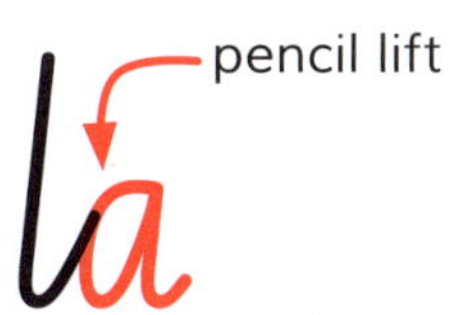

Take the exit of the first letter high, lift your pencil and drop in the next letter.

Practise dropping in the anti-clockwise letters in the words. The dots show where the drop-in joins are.

planets galaxy magnetic metallic mantle aqua heat rotate clouds

degrees volcanoes asteroids rotational terrestrial launch equal

accelerate wavelength equator descent weather ultraviolet radiation

Add dots to indicate where there would be drop-in joins when written in cursive.

astronaut lunar starlight meteoroid waxing

magnitude black hole elliptical mass radiation

A waxing moon is a phase of the lunar cycle.

Prove your dots were placed correctly by writing the words in cursive.

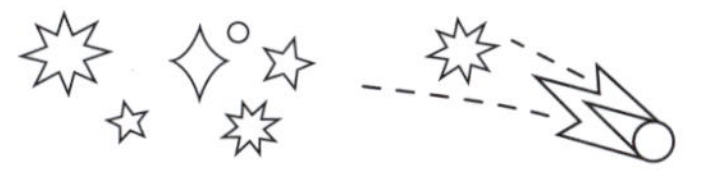

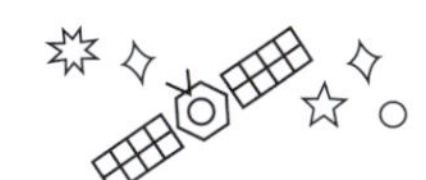

get.ga/PMWA102

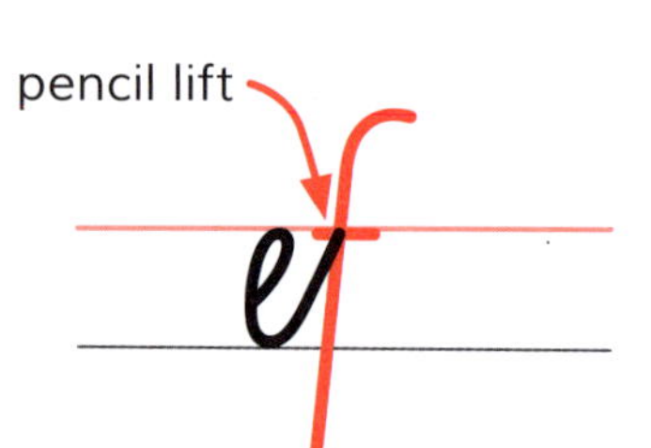

Remember: when dropping in 'f', extend the exit of the first letter, then lift your pencil to drop in 'f'. Make sure the crossbar and the exit flick meet at the body line.

Copy these letter pairs with drop-in joins to 'f'.

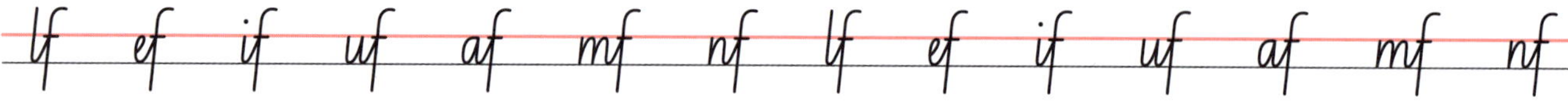

Copy the words. Take special care with your drop-in joins.

affect lift infrared effort spacecraft inflight

fifth difference lifesaving shelf infinite tuft

Write sentences using the words in the box. Take special care with your drop-in joins. Think of other words with drop-in joins to 'f', and write sentences using them.

spacecraft	lift	infrared	fifth

Horizontal joins to anti-clockwise letters

Remember: when making a horizontal join to anti–clockwise letters, some retracing is required.

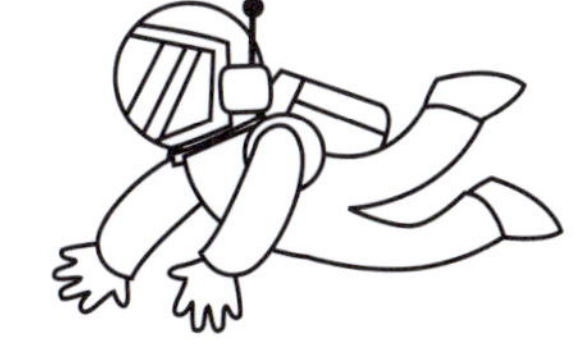

Copy these letter pairs with horizontal joins to anti-clockwise letters.

oa oc od og oo ra rc rd ro

va vo wa wc wd wo xa xc xo

Copy these words with horizontal joins to anti-clockwise letters.

rocket moon vacuum water Armstrong radio

wavelength Sea of Tranquillity astronaut dog module

Copy this story starter, being careful with your horizontal joins. Continue the story, using as many words with horizontal joins as possible.

On 16 July 1969, American astronaut Neil Armstrong

ISBN: 9780170416931

Horizontal joins to ascenders

Remember: when making a horizontal join to an ascender, sweep up, then retrace a little.

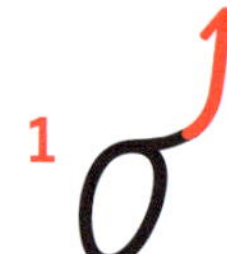

2

Copy these letter pairs with horizontal joins to ascenders.

ob of oh ok ol ot rb rf rh rk

rl rt vl wh wl wt wf xh xl xt

Copy these words.

virtual technology objective whole revolve exhaust

solar turbulence violence volcanic pavlova

twirl obscure observatory total starlight

absolute exhume axle lift off obviously

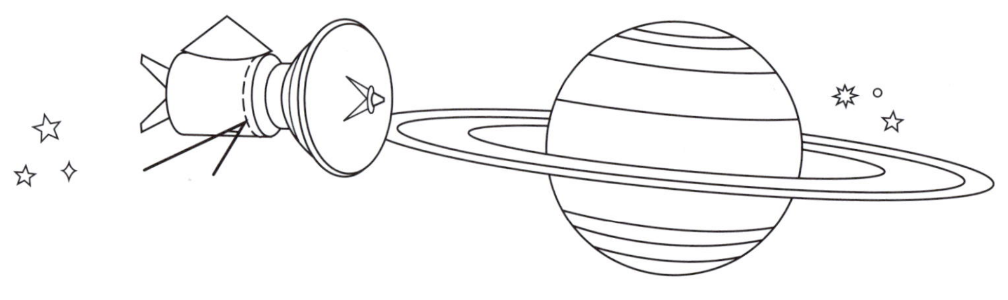

ISBN 9780170416931

Horizontal joins from 'f'

fu fi fa

TIP: Use the crossbar to join 'f' to the next letter.

fo fl

TIP: Retrace a little when joining from 'f' to 'o'. Retrace the downstroke of the letter 'l'.

Copy the words, being careful with your horizontal joins from 'f'.

flicker fan belt form float first function

factual perform reflex wonderful awfully

Astronauts in space need to eat special, highly nutritious food to keep them healthy for the strenuous tasks they complete. Imagine they could have one 'treat day' where they could also have some food they might like. Design a menu for them using the following foods.

fish favourite food tofu flan figs fondue
fudge fajitas flatbread feta seafood falafel

WATER

Breakfast:

Lunch:

Dinner:

Horizontal joins review

Take a letter from each box to make letter pairs with horizontal joins. Remember not to dip the join too far.

oc

o r v w x

to

a b c d g h i k l m
n o p r s t u v x y z

Copy these words, then underline the horizontal joins.

clothes astronaut formal outside move rocket

around protects dangers several ways vacuum

oxygen water sound dangerous moving orbit

covers possible cooling during primary world

Make new words by adding a letter or letters to these word endings with horizontal joins.

____oat ____og ____orn ____ood ____ook

____ork ____oon ____one ____ost ____oor

Self-assessment: Building fluency

Copy the text in your best cursive handwriting.

Jupiter is the fifth planet from the Sun and the largest
planet in our solar system. It is a gas giant, and may appear
to be hazy when viewed from an observatory. Four large,
luminous moons move in orbit around Jupiter, along with many
smaller moons. This amazing planet broadcasts radio waves
strong enough for scientific equipment on Earth to detect.

get.ga/PMWA103

Self-assessment

Rate your fluency and legibility.

☐ I need more practice.

☐ Good.

☐ Excellent!

Foundation printing

Revise the Foundation printing alphabet.

a b c d e f g h i j k l m n o p q r s t u v w x y z

Copy these words.

Ceres dwarf planet asteroid belt inner craters

Use the words above to complete the sentences. Then copy the text.

Ceres is a ________ ________. It is located in the ________ ________ between Mars and Jupiter. ________ is covered in many small ________. It is the only dwarf planet in the ________ solar system.

Copy the facts about dwarf planets.

Dwarf planets are smaller than planets.

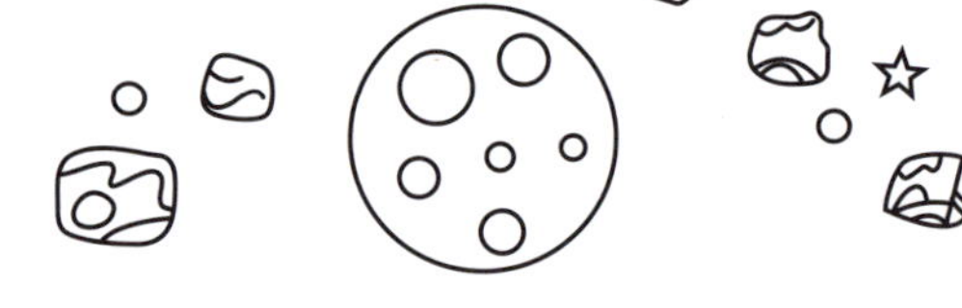

They are rounded objects that orbit the Sun.

Some dwarf planets have moons of their own.

Pluto is now called a dwarf planet, instead of a planet.

Capital letters

Revise your capital letters.

A B C D E F G H I J K L M N O P

Q R S T U V W X Y Z

Rewrite these words in all capital letters.

living working space food clothing exercise communicate
research zero gravity self-care daily mission dreams
snoring excitement motion nightmares wake hours

List the capital letters in the words above that have downstrokes.

List the capital letters in the words above that have a rounded shape.

List the capital letters in the words above that have diagonal lines.

Numerals

Add the missing numerals and numeral names to the table.

Planet	Diameter	Diameter in words
Mercury	4879 km	Four thousand, eight hundred and seventy-nine kilometres
Venus		Twelve thousand, one hundred and four kilometres
Earth	12 756 km	
Mars		Six thousand, seven hundred and ninety-two kilometres
Jupiter		One hundred and forty-two thousand, nine hundred and eighty-four kilometres
Saturn	120 536 km	
Uranus	51 118 km	
Neptune		Forty-nine thousand, five hundred and twenty-eight kilometres

Which planet is the largest? ______________________

Which planet is the smallest? ______________________

Which planet is most similar in size to Earth? ______________________

List the planets from smallest to largest. ______________________

____

Punctuation

Rewrite these jokes and add question marks.

Q: When do astronauts eat their sandwiches

A: At launch time!

Q: What kind of music can you hear in space

A: A Nep–tune.

Rewrite the text in cursive. Include quotation marks, and give each speaker a new line.

Do you think you will be famous when you grow up? the teacher asked her 10–year–old student. I don't know but I do want to learn to fly replied Neil Armstrong.

Double letter combinations

oss

double 's' from a horizontal join

iss

double 's' from a diagonal join

When writing double 's', make both letters look the same.

You can speed up double 'f' by using one crossbar.

Copy these words with double letters.

discussion mass pressure compress across airless

assembled difficult fluffy sufficient offline offering

offshore efficient moon books afternoon bedroom

meet greet sleet preen aggravate buggy shaggy

bigger blogger all small taller hilly ammunition

jamming dimmer dinner running scanner sunny

happy skipper chopping bopping ripped hopping

stirrer furry putty babysitter hitting flatten fittest

Rewrite these sentences, adding interesting adjectives where you can.
Remember to be careful with your double letter combinations.

The lunar buggy drove well on the surface of the Moon.

All the stars twinkled in the sky.

The comet appeared to be dimmer than when it was last seen.

Only the thinnest crescent of the Moon appeared in the evening.

Walking in zero gravity can feel a bit like hopping.

Astronauts are chosen from the fittest candidates.

get.ga/PMWA105

Classifying joins

Sort these letter pairs according to their correct join type.
Some letter pairs belong in more than one category.

cc ki ow wl vo ng rl co ac rs bb ph st
ew wh ot cq om il nd ol cr on sc br pa

Diagonal joins	Drop-in joins
Horizontal joins	**Horizontal joins to ascenders**
Fluency joins	**Fluency joins to ascenders**

Copy this sentence in cursive twice.

The five boxing wizards jumped over the lazy frog.

List the letter pairs from the sentence above that join diagonally.

List the letter pairs from the sentence above with drop-in joins.

List the letters from the sentence above that don't join.

Converting between scripts

Complete the table to practise printing, cursive and capital letters.

Printing	Cursive	Capital letters
Milky Way	Milky Way	
		UNIVERSE
solar system		
	planets	
Mercury		
	Venus	
Mars		
	asteroids	
Kuiper belt		
	satellites	
meteoroid		
	Earth	

Match each definition to a word from the table above. Write the answer in your preferred script.

- the red planet made up of dense rock: ______________________
- the galaxy that contains our solar system: ______________________
- a belt of small bodies beyond Neptune: ______________________
- spacecraft or astronomical bodies in orbit: ______________________
- the only planet known to support human life: ______________________
- the planet closest to the Sun: ______________________

Labelling timelines

Add labels from the box to the timeline. Use Foundation printing.

1969	First human on the Moon
1961	First human spaceflight
1971	First space probe to orbit Mars
1963	First woman in space
1957	First animal in orbit (Laika the dog)

A timeline of early space exploration

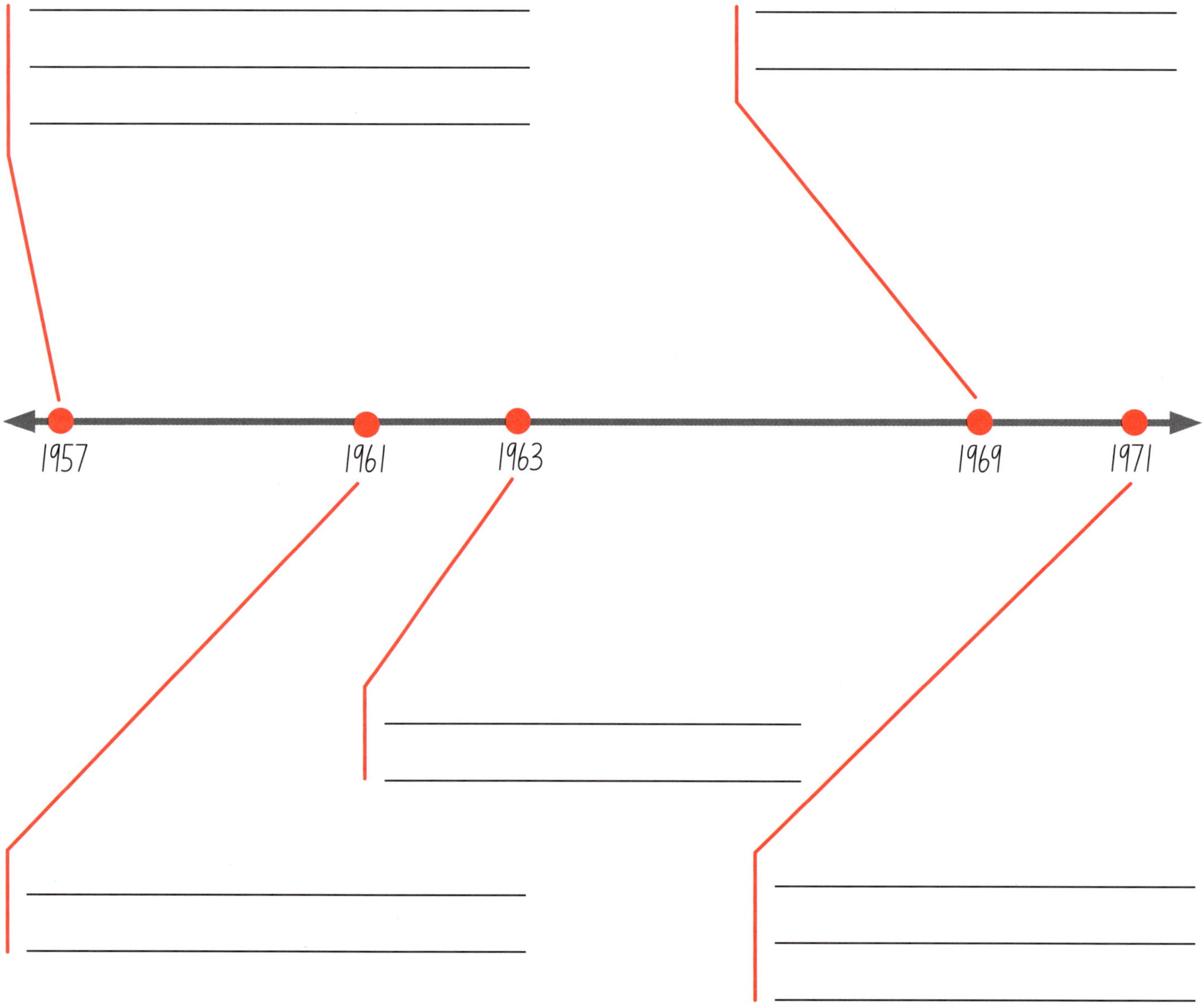

1957 1961 1963 1969 1971

Labelling diagrams

Label the diagram. Use Foundation printing.

Earth	Venus	Mercury	Uranus
Saturn	Jupiter	Mars	Neptune

The planets of our solar system

Now, write the names of the planets in cursive, starting with the planet closest to the Sun.

Legibility: Slope, spacing and size

get.ga/PMWA106

Trace and complete these words and patterns at different sizes.
Try to maintain a consistent slope.

science s

crater c

launch

llll ll

axis a

>>>>

ox ox ox

Copy the text, then check your spacing. Colour a small red square between each word.

The second planet from the Sun is Venus. Its surface temperature is 472°C. The size of Venus is similar to that of Earth. Venus has no moons or rings, and it rotates in the opposite direction to most other planets.

Copy these patterns to practise maintaining even spacing between letters.

ooo www eee

uuu mmm ulul

Look at the different versions of the word 'Neptune'. Circle the one that has the most appropriate letter spacing.

Neptune Neptune Neptune Neptune

Practise maintaining a consistent slope. Copy each word in the slope grid.

exoplanet

universe

terrestrial

atmosphere

habitable

telescope

galaxy

Circle the statement or statements that apply to you.

- These slope grids were easy to use.
- These slope grids were hard to use.
- These slope grids helped me keep a consistent slope.

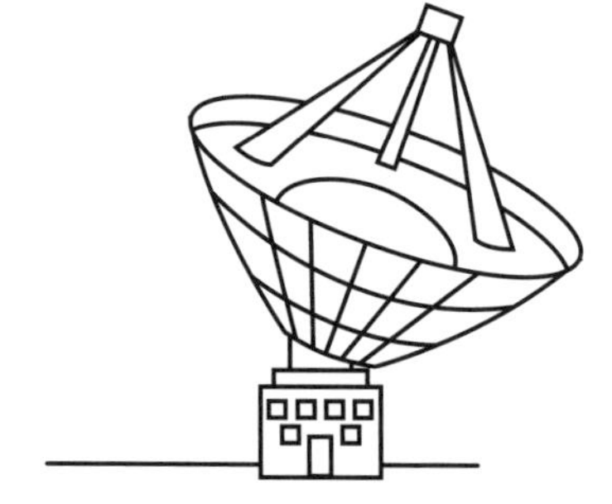

Self-assessment: Legibility – Slope, spacing and size

Copy the text. Remember to be careful with your slope, spacing and size.

Scientists originally believed that Earth was flat, and there are many historical maps representing this idea. Indeed, sailors used to worry that when they reached the edge of the world, they would fall off! Once astronomers were able to look at photos of Earth taken from outer space, they saw that our planet clearly has a spherical shape.

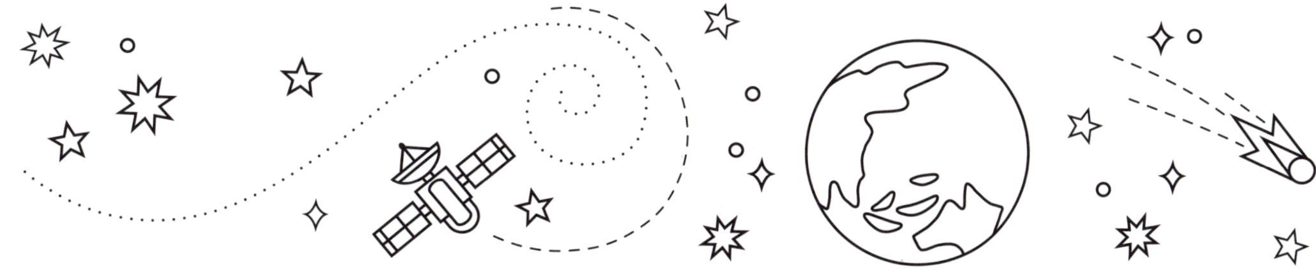

Self-assessment

Rate your slope, spacing and size.

They're inconsistent.

They're mostly consistent.

They're always consistent!

Speed loops from descenders

Adding a speed loop to the tail, or descender, of a letter can help you to write faster and with fluency. Make a loop and trail your pen or pencil up from the descender, crossing at the baseline.

galactic jump yonder

loop crosses at the baseline

TIP A speed loop is not needed if 'g', 'j' or 'y' is at the end of a word.

Copy these letter pairs and words with speed loops from 'g'.

gl ga gu gr gh ge gl ga gu gr

gravity age large guru green great grip

Copy these letter pairs and words with speed loops from 'j'.

ja ju jo ju je ji ja ju jo ju je ji

jaguar jumped join object adjust joy jest

Copy these letter pairs and words with speed loops from 'y'.

yr yo yu ye yi ya yr yo jo

year young yes lying myriad yapping yesterday

Speed loops to ascenders 'b', 'h', 'k' and 'l'

loops cross at the body line

ph ck

TIP Using speed loops when joining to 'b', 'h', 'k' and 'l' makes joining letters faster because there is less to retrace. These speed loops cross at the body line.

Copy these letter pairs and words with speed loops to 'b'.

rb ib mb ob ub bb lb ab rb ib

suburb bib comb lobby tub bulb bubble

Copy these letter pairs and words with speed loops to 'h'.

ch ph gh sh th oh ch ph gh sh

children graph shout thistle tough touch wish

Copy these letter pairs and words with speed loops to 'k'.

ek ok ck nk rk sk ak ek

speak plank knock ask quack deck shark walk

Copy these letter pairs and words with speed loops to 'l'.

al ol ul il rl tl sl pl wl gl

girl holly subtle pill enthral howl slender plate

black hole

A speed loop is not needed if 'b', 'h', 'k' or 'l' appears at the beginning of a word.

Rewrite the text in cursive, using speed loops in the correct places.

A black hole is a region in space where the force of gravity is so strong that light is not able to escape. Scientists can locate a black hole by observing its effect on stars and gases around it. The Sun does not have enough mass to become a black hole. At the end of its life, it will become a red giant. It will then burst the outer layers and become a planetary nebula. Finally, all that will be left of the Sun will be a white dwarf star.

Speed loops to and from 'f'

When 'f' is at the beginning of a word, use a tail speed loop and no crossbar.

Copy these letter pairs and words beginning with 'f'.

flare flight fumble faint fabric failure focus flexible

When 'f' is in the middle of a word, use both a head and a tail speed loop. This 'f' doesn't need a crossbar.

Copy these words with 'f' in the middle of the word.

beliefs perform unsafe reflex lift wonderful afterwards

awfully after before ruffle rafter shuffle therefore coffee

When 'f' is at the end of a word, use a head speed loop and include the crossbar.

Copy these letter pairs and words ending with 'f'.

rf uf lf of ef af rf uf lf of ef

lift off white dwarf staff stiff turf loaf puff leaf

Speed loops from 'z'

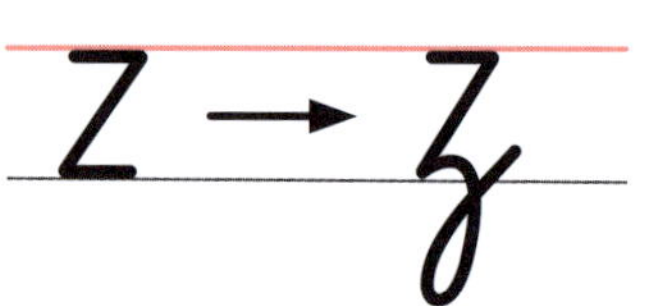

When you add a speed loop to 'z', the shape of the letter changes.

Copy the text.

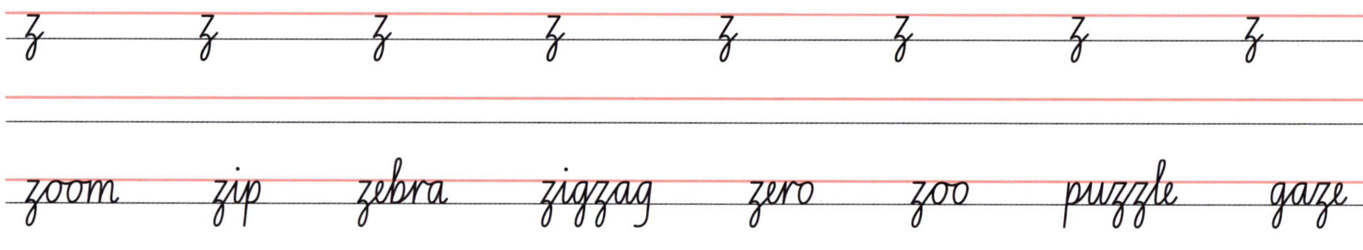

When 'z' is at the end of a word, no speed loop is required, but you still use the modified 'z'.

Copy these words.

fuzz fizz quiz buzz waltz quartz topaz whizz

Copy the text. Take special care with your speed loops from 'z'.

Three, two, one, zero! The space shuttle zoomed away from Earth

and zipped past the clouds towards outer space.

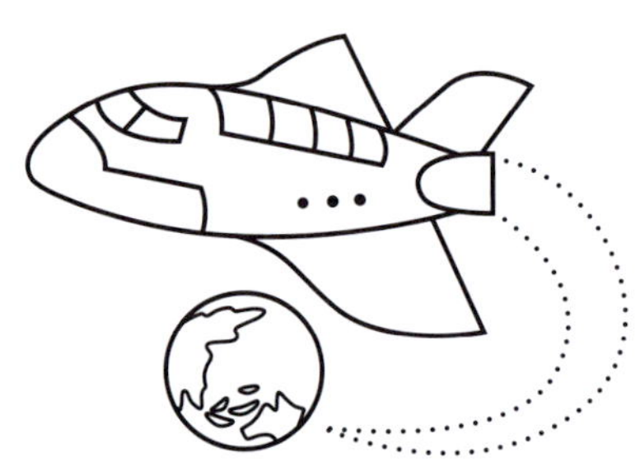

Practising speed loops

Practise using speed loops in regular writing lines. Copy the text.

Astronomers are very interested in dwarf planets, which are mostly located in the outer solar system. In 2015, two NASA space probes visited dwarf planets: 'Dawn' reached Ceres, and 'New Horizons' reached Pluto. The planet Ceres is located in the asteroid belt. It is so little that it is classified as both a dwarf planet and an asteroid. Because dwarf planets are small, their gravity is not sufficient to attract or push away smaller bodies.

Scientists have long been enthralled by the effects of gravity. It is a force great enough to affect the speed of a space shuttle as it lifts off from Earth and zooms into outer space.

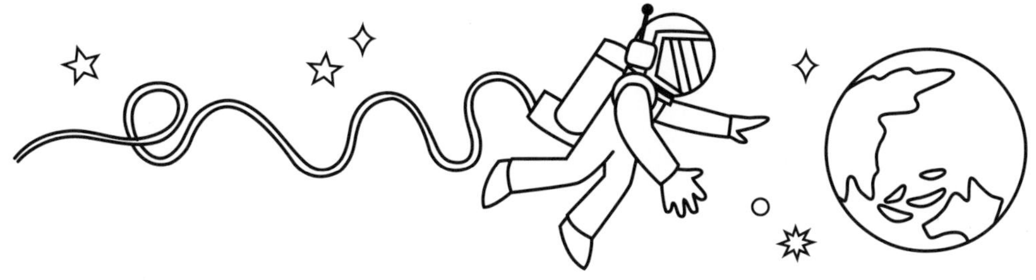

get.ga/PMWA107

Speed and legibility

It is important to balance speed and accurate letter formation so your writing is quick and legible.

Work with a partner to find out how many times you can write the word 'eclipse' in cursive in one minute.

eclipse

______ times

Now write the word again. This time, write as neatly as you can. How many times did you write it in one minute?

eclipse

______ times

Now find out how many times you can write the word neatly in Foundation printing in one minute.

eclipse

______ times

My most legible script when writing at speed is: ____________________

Rewrite the text in cursive. Take special care to add speed loops correctly where required.

Neptune is fresco blue in colour and is named after the god of the sea in Roman legend. It is a cold, dark planet with the strongest winds in the solar system. Neptune is one of the gas giants, and the furthest planet from the Sun. Neptune has 13 known moons. It has only been photographed up close once in space history, when the spacecraft Voyager 2 zoomed there to visit.

Peer review

Ask your partner to give you some feedback on how well you wrote the text above. Ask them to notice how carefully you formed your speed loops.

2 stars (two things you did well)

I wish (a way for you to improve)

Handwriting in context

Draw a mind map that includes some outer space concepts covered in this book. You may use Foundation printing or cursive, but do your best to be as neat as possible, and to practise the handwriting skills you have learnt.

outer space

Independent writing activity

Imagine that you meet Neil Armstrong after he becomes the first person to walk on the Moon. Write five questions you would like to ask him.

Imagine all the planets in our solar system can support human life. Write a text explaining which planet you would like to visit and why.

Teacher observation guide

Student is: left-handed ☐ right-handed ☐

Student demonstrates correct posture, paper position and pencil grip. ☐

Student forms the NSW Foundation style alphabet with accuracy. ☐

Student forms capital letters with accuracy. ☐

Student forms numerals with accuracy. ☐

Student forms the following joins with accuracy:

- diagonal joins ☐
- drop-in joins ☐
- horizontal joins ☐
- fluency joins ☐
- speed loops ☐

Student can convert between scripts. ☐

Student uses 9 mm regular writing lines with accuracy. ☐

Student has an understanding of the factors that influence legibility (slope, spacing, size, speed). ☐

Student uses NSW Foundation style cursive confidently. ☐

Student is progressing towards a fluent and legible personal handwriting style. ☐

Notes:

....

....

....

Date:

....

CERTIFICATE

get.ga/PMWC100